GAL
CENGAG ......ng

Short Stories for Students, Volume 12

Staff

Editor: Jennifer Smith.

Contributing Editors: Anne Marie Hacht, Michael L. LaBlanc, Ira Mark Milne, Elizabeth Thomason.

Managing Editor, Literature Content: Dwayne D. Hayes.

Managing Editor, Literature Product: David Galens.

Publisher, Literature Product: Mark Scott.

Content Capture: Joyce Nakamura, *Managing Editor*.Michelle Poole, *Associate Editor*.

Research: Victoria B. Cariappa, *Research Manager*.Cheryl Warnock, *Research Specialist*.Tamara Nott, Trade A. Richardson, *Research Associates*.Nicodemus Ford, Sarah Genik, Timothy Lehnerer, Ron Morelli, *Research Assistants*.

Permissions: Maria Franklin, *Permissions Manager*. Jacqueline Jones, Julie Juengling, *Permissions Assistants*.

Manufacturing: Mary Beth Trimper, *Manager, Composition and Electronic Prepress*.Evi Seoud, *Assistant Manager, Composition Purchasing and Electronic Prepress*.Stacy Melson, *Buyer*.

Imaging and Multimedia Content Team: Barbara Yarrow, *Manager*.Randy Bassett, *Imaging Supervisor*.Robert Duncan, Dan Newell, *Imaging Specialists*.Pamela A. Reed, *Imaging Coordinator*.Leitha Etheridge-Sims, Mary Grimes, David G. Oblender, *Image Catalogers*.Robyn V. Young, *Project Manager*.Dean Dauphinais, *Senior Image Editor*. Kelly A. Quin, *Image Editor*.

Product Design Team: Kenn Zorn, *Product Design Manager*.Pamela A. E. Galbreath, *Senior Art Director*.Michael Logusz, *Graphic Artist*.

Copyright Notice

The Metamorphosis

Franz Kafka

1915

Introduction

"The Metamorphosis" is probably the best-known story written by the Czech-born German-Jewish writer Franz Kafka, ranking with his two novel-length masterpieces, *The Trial* and *The Castle*.

First published in 1915 in German (under the title "Die Verwandlung"), "The Metamorphosis" was written over the course of three weeks in November and December 1912. Kafka at one point contemplated publishing it along with two other stories about father-son relations in a collection to be called *Sons*, but later decided to issue it on its own. It was first translated into English in 1936, and has been translated several times since.

The haunting story of a man transformed into an insect has attracted numerous commentators, who while agreeing on the high quality and importance of the story disagree strongly about what it means. Freudian, Marxist, existentialist, and religious interpretations have all been proposed, and there has been debate over whether Gregor Samsa, the man-turned-insect, symbolizes the human condition.

It is generally agreed, however, that the story portrays a world that is hostile and perhaps absurd and that major themes in the story include father-son antagonism (perhaps reflecting Kafka's difficult relationship with his own father), alienation at work, isolation, and self-sacrifice.

The story is sometimes praised for its symmetrical, three-part structure and its use of black humor, and its symbols (such as the lady in furs and the music played by Gregor's sister) are sometimes puzzled over, but what makes the story memorable is the central situation of the transformation of a man into an insect and the image of the man-insect lying on his back helplessly waving his little insect legs in the air.

Born in Prague in 1883 into a Jewish family, Kafka lived the life of an isolated loner. He never married, though he was engaged several times, and he lived most of his life in his parents' house. He had a difficult relationship with his businessman father, which he described at length in "Letter to His Father," and had difficulty writing at home amidst the noise and distractions of a household that included three younger sisters and servants.

After graduating from university, Kafka took a job in an insurance company, which he hated; he later found a more congenial position in the Workmen' s Accident Insurance Institute, but still felt that his full-time job interfered with his writing. He eventually had to give up his full-time job because of illness: throughout his life he was prone to a variety of real and imaginary illnesses, and became a vegetarian in an attempt to improve his constitution. He died of tuberculosis a month before his forty-first birthday, June 3, 1924.

Although Prague was a Czech city, it had a sizable German minority, and the Jews of Prague tended to identify with the Germans. The Kafka family was no exception, and Kafka's first language, and the language he wrote in, was German. He began writing at an early age, but destroyed most of his childhood works and remained very critical of his writings all his life. He had to be encouraged, most notably by his friend and fellow writer Max Brod, to keep on writing and publishing. "The Metamorphosis" was one work that he did think worth publishing, though he was critical even of it when he first completed it.

At the end of his life, Kafka felt so negative about his works that he instructed Brod to burn his unpublished manuscripts and make sure that his published works were never republished. Brod, however, ignored these instructions and brought out posthumous editions of two of Kafka's previously unknown masterpieces: *The Trial* and *The Castle*.

Plot Summary

Part I

As the story opens, Gregor Samsa has already turned into a gigantic insect. He notices this, but does not seem to find it horrifying or even that unusual, merely an inconvenience or perhaps a delusion. He worries mainly that he has overslept and will be late for work. He also thinks to himself about how unpleasant his job is and how he would have quit long before now if not for having to earn money to pay off his parents' debts.

Gregor's parents and his sister knock at his locked bedroom door and ask if something is the matter. Gregor tries to answer, but his voice sounds strange, like a "horrible twittering squeak." He is also unable at first to control his new insect body well enough to get out of bed; his little insect legs wave helplessly as he lies on his back.

The chief clerk from Gregor's job arrives, demanding to know why Gregor has not shown up for work. This irritates Gregor, who thinks it is excessive of his firm to send such a high-level person to inquire into such a minor deviation from duty. When the chief clerk, speaking through the door to the still unseen Gregor, criticizes him and hints that he may lose his job, Gregor becomes even more upset and makes a long speech in his defense which none of the listeners can understand. "That was no human voice," says the chief clerk. Gregor's mother thinks he must be ill and sends his sister, Grete, for a doctor. Gregor's father sends the servant girl for a locksmith.

Gregor meanwhile has decided that the best thing will be to show himself. With great difficulty, using his toothless insect jaws, he turns the key in the lock and then pulls the door open. At the sight of him, the chief clerk backs away, Gregor's mother falls to the floor, and his father first shakes his fist and then begins to cry.

Gregor is anxious to keep the chief clerk from leaving and spreading bad reports about him— Gregor's main concern is still the possible loss of his job—but the clerk rushes out, yelling "Ugh!" and his father shoos Gregor back into his room.

Part II

Gregor in this section of the story becomes more and more insect-like. He discovers that he is most comfortable under the sofa and comes to enjoy crawling up the walls and hanging from the ceiling. He also learns that he no longer likes fresh food, but prefers the half-decayed scraps that his sister leaves for him. His sister is now the only one who takes care of him, but even she seems disgusted by him. Realizing this, Gregor arranges a sheet in front of the sofa to hide himself from her.

Thinking that it might be best for Gregor if he had more room in which to crawl, Gregor's sister decides to remove his furniture and gets her mother to help. Gregor thinks this is a good idea too until he hears his mother say that perhaps after all it is wrong: it is signaling to Gregor that the family has given up all hope that he will return to human form. Suddenly feeling very attached to the symbols of his human past, Gregor rushes out from his hiding place under the sofa and decides to defend his belongings, especially the picture on his wall of a lady in furs, which he climbs on top of. When his mother sees him, she faints, and the ensuing confusion ends with Gregor's father attacking Gregor by bombarding him with apples, one of which seriously wounds him. It is Gregor who now faints, but before he loses consciousness he sees his half-undressed mother rush into his father's arms.

Part III

Without Gregor's income to support them, the other family members, who formerly did not work, now all take jobs and as a result complain of being overworked and tired as well as of being uniquely afflicted—presumably referring to their having to take care of Gregor. Gregor meanwhile is still suffering from being struck by the apple; in fact, the apple has lodged in his back, no one has bothered to remove it, and the area around it has become inflamed. Gregor also feels neglected and loses his appetite, and has to put up with having his room turned into a dumping area after the family takes in three lodgers. As well, he is tormented by the new charwoman the family hires to replace the live-in servant they could no longer afford.

One evening Gregor's sister plays the violin for her parents and the lodgers. Gregor is greatly affected by the music and thinks it is opening a path for him to some unknown sort of nourishment. He ventures out of his room, intending to reach his sister, all the while fantasizing about getting her to move into his room with her violin, where he would protect her from all intruders and kiss her on the neck.

When the lodgers see Gregor and for the first time realize that they are sharing a house with such a creature, they instantly give notice and say they will sue for damages. Gregor's sister says it is time they got rid of Gregor; he is driving away their lodgers and generally persecuting his family, and he is not really Gregor anymore, just a creature.

Gregor retreats to his room, feeling weak and thinking that he must disappear as his sister wanted. He dies that night and is disposed of the next day by the charwoman. His death seems to energize the family, especially Mr. Samsa, who stops being deferential to the three lodgers and instead orders them out of the house.

The story ends with the three surviving Samsas on an excursion into the countryside thinking about their prospects. They decide that things are not so bad: their jobs are actually promising, and Grete has blossomed into an attractive young woman for whom her parents will soon find a husband.

Characters

Charwoman

Hired by the Samsas to replace their live-in servant, the charwoman is a tough old woman who, unlike the other characters, is neither horrified nor frightened by Gregor's insect form. She even refers to Gregor affectionately as "the old dung beetle" and less affectionately threatens him with a chair. She is the one who discovers that Gregor has died and who cheerfully disposes of his body.

Chief Clerk

The chief clerk from Gregor's firm comes to the Samsa house to find out why Gregor has not shown up for work. When Gregor delays coming out of his room, the clerk criticizes him for poor work performance and reports that the head of the firm suspects Gregor of embezzling funds. When Gregor finally emerges, the clerk flees in horror.

Gregor's father

See Mr. Samsa

Gregor's mother

See Mrs. Samsa

Gregor's sister

See Grete Samsa

Gregor Samsa

Gregor Samsa, the protagonist of the story, is a self-sacrificing, dutiful young man who is mysteriously transformed into a giant insect as the story begins. He lives with his parents and his sister, whom he has been supporting by working as a travelling salesman, a job he very much dislikes, but which he devotes his life to: he seems to have no close friends and no social life. There are hints of repressed resentment in Gregor's attitude toward his family; he seems to feel that his sacrifices for them have not been properly appreciated. And despite his dutiful nature, he does not seem very close to his family, except for his sister, whose musical studies he has been planning to finance.

After his transformation, Gregor's character changes somewhat: on two occasions, he puts his own desires ahead of what others want, first when he tries to defend his belongings in opposition to his sister's plan to remove them, and second when he seeks to obtain the mysterious nourishment associated with his sister's violin playing. In the end, however, he reverts to his self-sacrificing ways by willingly going to his death because his family wants to be rid of him.

Grete Samsa

Grete Samsa, usually referred to in the story as Gregor's sister, is the family member Gregor seems closest to and is the one who takes care of him after his transformation. Even she seems disgusted by his new form, however, and she is the one who at the end demands that he be got rid of.

Before the transformation, the seventeen-year-old Grete leads an idle life and is regarded by her parents as "a somewhat useless daughter." After the transformation, she becomes a sales clerk as well as taking on the responsibility of caring for Gregor. Tired out by all these new duties, she begins to neglect Gregor, but is furious when her mother cleans Gregor's room, seeing this action as an invasion of her domain.

Twice Grete does things that lead Gregor to leave his room, for which he suffers serious consequences. First, her decision to remove Gregor's furniture leads to a confrontation in the living room that ends with Gregor being seriously injured. Later her violin playing lures Gregor into the living room again, provoking the conflict that leads to his death. She is also the one who argues the most strongly for getting rid of Gregor. After Gregor's death, Grete blooms, and her parents think she is ready for a husband.

Mr. Samsa

Mr. Samsa, referred to only as Gregor's father until Gregor's death, is a failed businessman who has been idle for five years, living off what Gregor earns. He seems quite antagonistic to his son, fierce toward him, though at the same time weak: when he first sees the transformed Gregor, he shakes a fist at him, but then breaks down and cries.

It is the fierceness that dominates, however. The first two times Gregor ventures out of his room, his father forces him back in, the first time brandishing a walking stick and a newspaper at him, the second time bombarding him with apples. He does injury to Gregor both times.

After Gregor's transformation, Mr. Samsa is also transformed; before, he was a sluggish man who hardly ever got dressed and who could barely walk; now he is a bank messenger in a smart uniform who is reluctant ever to take it off. He is still weak in some ways, though, waiting cap in hand on the lodgers, for instance, until Gregor's death, at which point he becomes invigorated and is able to stand up to both the lodgers and the charwoman.

Media Adaptations

- In 1987, there was a British television adaptation of "The Metamorphosis." *Called Metamorphosis* and starring Tim Roth as Gregor Samsa, it was written by Steven Berkoff and directed by Jim Goddard.

- Steven Berkoff also wrote a stage adaptation of the story, which was first performed at the Round House in London in 1969 with him in the role of Gregor Samsa. Between 1969 and 1992, there were nine productions of Berkoff s adaptation, including ones in 1986 at the Mermaid in London with Tim Roth, in 1988 in Paris with Roman Polanski, in 1989 in New York with Mikhail Baryshnikov, and in 1992 in Tokyo. The text of the adaptation can be found in *"The Trial"; "Metamorphosis"; "In the Penal Colony": Three Theatre Adaptations from Franz Kafka* by Berkoff (Oxford, 1988). Berkoff discusses the various theatre productions in his book, *Meditations on "Metamorphosis"*(Faber, 1995).

- In 1976, a Swedish film directed by Ivo Dvorak was made of "The

Metamorphosis" under the title *Forvandlingen.*There have also been two short animated versions of the story, one a 1977 Canadian film directed by Caroline Leaf and called *The Metamorphosis of Mr. Samsa,* and the other an eight-minute-long 1999 Spanish production directed by Charlie Ramos.

- There is a 1993 British short film called *Franz Kafka's It's a Wonderful Life.*This odd production is not an adaptation of "The Metamorphosis," but it does provide a fanciful, fictional account of how Kafka supposedly wrote the story, showing him as being constantly interrupted while he tries to decide what sort of creature Gregor Samsa will be transformed into. Written and directed by Peter Capaldi, it stars Richard E. Grant as Kafka and Crispin Letts as Gregor Samsa.

- Another odd production is the 1989 film called *Nabokov On Kafka: "The Metamorphosis,"* directed by Peter Medak, in which Christopher Plummer plays the author Vladimir Nabokov giving a lecture on "The Metamorphosis."

- "The Metamorphosis" was recorded on audiocassette in 1994. Read by

Alan Hewitt, the cassette version, on two tapes, is three hours long and is unabridged.

Mrs. Samsa

Mrs. Samsa, who is referred to as Gregor's mother throughout except after Gregor dies, is perhaps the character most sympathetic to Gregor, and the most willing to come to his defense. When something first seems wrong with Gregor, she assumes he is ill and wants to send for the doctor. When the chief clerk is being critical of Gregor, she assures him that Gregor is a very hard worker. When Mr. Samsa throws apples at Gregor, Mrs. Samsa rushes to intervene.

On the other hand, Mrs. Samsa cannot really stand to look at her son in his transformed state: the first two times she does so she screams and faints. She is also not strong enough to defend Gregor successfully: she allows Grete to overrule her on whether to remove Gregor's furniture; and when Grete and Mr. Samsa begin to discuss getting rid of Gregor, Mrs. Samsa has an asthmatic fit and is unable to intervene.

The Three Lodgers

Arriving in the Samsa household near the end of the story, the three lodgers are serious gentlemen who acquire power over the household. They always act together, as if they were a single character, though they do have a leader ("the middle lodger"). It is their request that leads to Grete' s violin concert in the living room. When they discover Gregor, they give notice and threaten to sue, but when Mr. Samsa orders them out they leave quietly.

Themes

Alienation at Work

One of the themes of the story is the unpleasantness of work. Gregor Samsa hates his job as a travelling salesman, but must continue doing it to pay off his parents' debts. There is no suggestion that he gets any job satisfaction; all he talks about is how exhausting the job is, how irritating it is to be always travelling: making train connections, sleeping in strange beds, always dealing with new people and thus never getting the chance to make good friends, and so forth. Moreover, it turns out that Gregor works for a firm that does not trust its employees at all: because he is late this one day, the chief clerk shows up to check on him and begins hinting that he is suspected of embezzling funds and may very well be fired. It also seems that Gregor's co-workers dislike him because he is on the road so often; they gossip about him and the other travelling salesmen, making unfounded complaints such as that they make lots of money and just enjoy themselves. Work is hell, the story seems to suggest.

Father-Son Antagonism

Life at home, according to the story, is no paradise either. In particular, Gregor seems to have a difficult relationship with his father. The very first time Gregor's father is seen he is making a fist, albeit just to knock on Gregor's door. Soon after, however, he makes a fist more in earnest: when he first sees Gregor in his insect form, he shakes his fist at him and glares at him fiercely. Later he attacks him with a newspaper and a walking stick, and, later still, bombards him with apples, causing him serious injury. He is also not above making sarcastic comments, suggesting for instance that Gregor's room is untidy. And it turns out that he has deceived Gregor about the family finances, thus needlessly extending the length of Gregor's employment at the hateful travelling salesman's job. Finally, he does not seem particularly appreciative of the money Gregor has been bringing in; he is content to live off his son's labor, but Gregor feels there was "no special uprush of warm feeling" about it.

Topics for Further Study

- Depending on the translation and the commentator, Gregor is described variously as an insect, a bug, a beetle, a cockroach, a louse, and a piece of vermin. Is it possible to say precisely what sort of creature he turns into?

- What are the advantages and disadvantages of turning into a bug the way Gregor does?

- Music is sometimes identified with the spiritual realm. On the other hand, it is sometimes linked to the animal kingdom as something that appeals even to nonhuman species. How does music, especially Grete's violin playing, function in this story?

- To what extent is "The Metamorphosis" part of the existentialist tradition in literature exemplified by the works of such writers as Jean-Paul Sartre, Albert Camus, and Eugene Ionesco?

- What does Gregor die of? His wound? Starvation? Self-starvation? A broken heart? A desire to die? Who is responsible for his death? Is Kakfa being deliberately ambiguous on this issue? If so, why?

Gregor's disappointment over the lack of appreciation is one of the few critical thoughts he thinks about his father. He also thinks briefly that the money his father hid from him could have been used to free him from his job sooner, but he quickly dismisses the thought by saying that no doubt his father knew best. In short, the antagonism as portrayed in the story is mostly one-way: the father abuses the son, but the son suppresses his angry responses and accepts his downtrodden state.

Betrayal

The one person Gregor feels close to is his sister, and she at first seems like the one most attentive to his needs. She brings him his food and cleans his room, and even her plan to remove Gregor's furniture, which he objects to, seems well-meant: she thinks he needs more room in his insect state to crawl around. After a while, she begins neglecting Gregor. When he tries to approach her one last time, she turns on him viciously, falsely accusing him of wanting to kick the rest of the family out of the house, saying that he is not really Gregor but a creature that must be got rid of. The story seems to be suggesting that no one is to be trusted.

Isolation and Self-Sacrifice

Gregor seems to have no close friends at work or elsewhere, and no romantic attachments; he is not very close with his family, except for his sister who it turns out cannot be trusted; he seems to lead a lonely, isolated life even before his transformation, and the transformation reinforces his situation. As an insect, he cannot communicate at all, and he is forced to stay in his room; he is cut off almost entirely from the rest of humanity.

As an insect, he can still hear, however, so he knows what others want, but they cannot know what he wants. This seems an apt situation for Gregor to end up in, because his life even before his transformation seems to have been one of catering to others' needs while suppressing his own.

Escaping

Although in some ways the transformation reinforces Gregor's situation, in other ways becoming an insect is a way for him to escape his unhappy life. No longer will he have to work at his burdensome job; instead, he can spend his days scurrying around his room, something he seems to enjoy. One of the themes is the joy of escaping from one's responsibilities.

Seizing Power

Although this is not a route Gregor is able to pursue successfully, the story does indicate that some people are able to reverse the power relations in their lives. Gregor seems able only to remain downtrodden or to escape to insectdom; but his father is able to overthrow the domination of the three lodgers and recapture the authority in his house.

Interestingly, he can only do this after Gregor himself, the self-sacrificing, downtrodden one, is dead, perhaps suggesting that the presence of a self-sacrificing person drains those around him.

Style

Point of View

The story is told in the third person but is for the most part limited to Gregor's point of view. Only his thoughts and feelings are presented, and most of the events are seen through his eyes. The point seems to be to present a picture of Gregor and the world as he understands it, both before and after his metamorphosis. This does not necessarily mean that all of Gregor's judgements are to be accepted; on the contrary, Kafka uses irony and black comedy to indicate that Gregor is at times misled, for instance in thinking he can still go to the office even after becoming an insect and, more sadly, in thinking his family is putting his interests first.

Of course, after Gregor's death, the point of view has to shift; it becomes simply impersonal third-person narration, remaining on the outside of the surviving characters, not revealing their thoughts and feelings the way Gregor's were revealed earlier. Interestingly, Gregor's parents are now referred to impersonally as Mr. and Mrs. Samsa; earlier, when the story was being told from Gregor's point of view, they were invariably referred to as Gregor's father and Gregor's mother. The point of this shift seems to be to emphasize that Gregor is not just gone but forgotten.

Setting

The story has a very constricted setting; almost all the events take place within the Samsa house, mostly in Gregor's room, reflecting the fact that Gregor is essentially a prisoner. The room itself is small and, by the end, unclean. Gregor can see outside, but mostly what he sees is an overcast sky, rain, fog, and a gray hospital building; when his eyesight fades, he cannot even see the hospital, and the world beyond his room appears to him to be a gray desert.

The gloominess of this setting begins to change near the end. There is heavy rain, but the narrator suggests it might be a sign of spring. This is when Gregor is still alive. However, the truly decisive change in the setting occurs only after Gregor's death. For the first time, the story leaves the house, following the surviving Samsas into the countryside, where the sun shines on them as they cheerfully plan their future.

Structure

The story is divided into three parts, each one culminating in a foray by Gregor outside his room. The first two parts end when Gregor is forced back into his room. In part three, Gregor is again forced to return to his room; however, this part differs from the other two in that it does not end with Gregor's return, but contains a coda describing events of the next day.

Flashbacks and other Narrative Devices

Most of the story consists of extended scenes. All of part one is the scene that unfolds when Gregor awakes to find himself an insect; the last section of part two is the extended scene that begins when Gregor's sister and mother enter Gregor's room to remove his furniture; and the bulk of part three consists of two linked scenes: the violin concert that leads to Gregor's death and the scene that begins the next day with the discovery of his body, and that ends with the excursion to the countryside.

Only a small part of the story consists of summaries: most notably the passages near the beginning of each of the last two parts, which recount Gregor's typical activities, explain how he gets fed and informed, and report on how the family copes with the loss of Gregor's income.

Kafka also uses brief flashbacks to explain how Gregor came to be supporting his family and to contrast the current behavior of Gregor's father with how he behaved in the past.

Symbols

Kafka uses some obvious and not-so-obvious symbols in the story. Some symbols even the characters recognize as such: for instance, the furniture in Gregor's room, which his mother is reluctant to remove because of its association with

Gregor's human past; to remove the furniture is to declare symbolically that Gregor is no longer human and will never be human again.

Other symbols are less easy to understand. The recurrent use of the number three, for instance (three parts to the story, three doors to Gregor's room, three lodgers, three other family members), seems significant, but of what it is not clear. The fact that Gregor's father insists on wearing his uniform so long that it becomes greasy also seems significant but unclear; to wear a smart uniform instead of a bathrobe seems at first an indication of the father's increasing strength, but to wear it so long that it becomes greasy seems to indicate weakness again. It is also not entirely clear what the significance is of the picture of a carefree Gregor in a lieutenant's uniform: does it suggest that he once had a more satisfying existence, before becoming stuck in his boring job?

The picture of the lady in furs, which Gregor presses against when his belongings are taken away, seems to be some sort of romantic or sexual symbol, representing the limited nature of Gregor's romantic life. The music that draws Gregor seems to have a spiritual significance—or does it, on the contrary, suggest (as Gregor himself says) something animallike? The appearance of the butcher's boy at the end could be a symbol of returning life—or is it death? And the sunshine at the end also speaks of life, though it is a life dependent on Gregor's death, a life open to the Samsas only because they have got rid of Gregor.

Of course, the central symbol of the story is Gregor's insect form itself. What does it signify for a man to be turned into a giant bug? Is Kafka suggesting that this is the human condition? Is it the condition of only some humans? And what is that condition? Disgusting and ineffectual, or somehow positive?

Historical Context

Socio-Economic Background

For most of Kafka's lifetime, his home town of Prague was a Czech city within a German-speaking empire, the Austro-Hungarian Empire. Only at the end of World War I did that Empire disappear, leading to the creation of an independent Czechoslovakia. But in 1912, when Kafka was writing "The Metamorphosis," the Czechs had not yet won their independence, and despite its Czech majority, Prague was dominated by a German-speaking elite. Recognizing where the power lay in the city, the Jews of Prague tended to identify with the German minority rather than with the Czech majority; the Czechs therefore considered the Jews to be part of the German community, but the Germans themselves did not. As a result, it was easy for the Jews to feel that they did not fit in anywhere.

In general, Prague was a city of ethnic tensions, primarily between Czechs and Germans and between Czechs and Jews. In 1897, when Kafka was fourteen, the tensions erupted into anti-Semitic riots started by the Czechs. Thus Kafka would have grown up knowing hatred and hostility as well as the difficulty of fitting in.

Compare & Contrast

- **1840-1920s:** Kafka writes at a time when the drudgery of work is becoming a serious issue. Long hours at boring jobs create alienation. And tyrannical employers like Gregor's are the norm.

  Twentieth Century: Computers and other advances have allowed for more flexibility for employees, including flex time and telecommuting. Since computers can handle some of the more tedious and repetitious aspects of work, work for some may also be more intellectually stimulating. Also, the trend now is to promote friendlier employer-employee interactions. However, there are new employment problems today, and it is doubtful that the sort of work alienation depicted in Kafka's story has been eliminated altogether.

- **1840-1920s:** In Kafka's day, it is common for reasonably well-off families to employ full-time live-in servants to cook and clean and do other menial chores.

  Twentieth Century: Full-time servants are almost unheard of now, replaced primarily by labor-saving devices.

- **1840-1920s:** Kafka's "The

Metamorphosis" depicts a troubled father-son relationship that seems to reflect Kafka's own relationship with his father. Such troubled relationships may be widespread, inasmuch as during this time Sigmund Freud develops his theory of the Oedipus complex, which takes as its starting point the existence of a fundamental antagonism between fathers and sons.

Twentieth Century: The theory of the Oedipus complex has come under criticism, and the relationship of fathers and sons is often celebrated today. However, it would be hard to argue that the antagonisms described by Freud and Kafka do not exist.

- **1840-1920s:** Kafka's "The Metamorphosis" assumes that the insect is repulsive, suggesting that in Kafka's day it would be hard to have any positive feelings towards a bug.

  Twentieth Century: Perhaps in an era that produces movies that glamorize insects, like *A Bug's Life,* and which prides itself on ecological awareness and understanding of the importance of all orders of creatures, there is a more positive attitude towards bugs. However, it is hard to imagine that there would be much less horror today than a century ago at the idea of a man being changed into a cockroach.

Economically, the late nineteenth century marked the culmination of the Industrial Revolution in Europe. Industrial development was not as advanced in the Austro-Hungarian Empire as elsewhere in Europe, but within the Empire, Prague was one of the most advanced and prosperous cities. However, along with the prosperity created by the new industrialism came dislocation and disruption of the old ways, largely as a result of the shift of large numbers of people from the countryside to the city. Industrialization also meant the appearance of large numbers of jobs, for both factory and office workers, which were pure drudgery. And as if recognizing the need to train people for such jobs, the school system enforced a system of rote learning that seemed relentlessly joyless—at least it seemed joyless to young Kafka, who hated school, just as he hated his first full-time job.

Cultural Background

Prague was a cultured city, full of newspapers, theatres, and coffeehouses where avant-garde literary types could discuss the latest intellectual fashions. Kafka was a regular at two of these coffeehouses, the Arco and the Louvre, and through the discussions there may have been introduced to new philosophical ideas. He was certainly familiar with the newly published works of Sigmund Freud, referring to Freud in his diary not long before writing "The Metamorphosis." However, he was no Freudian disciple and wrote negatively of psychoanalytic theory. He was perhaps more in tune with the major nineteenth-century writers (such as Fyodor Dostoevsky, Friedrich Nietzsche, and Soren Kierkegaard) who wrote pessimistically of life in a meaningless or hostile universe, anticipating twentieth-century existentialism, a movement with which Kafka is sometimes associated.

In the year before writing "The Metamorphosis," Kafka became familiar with a Jewish theatre troupe that visited Prague and put on performances in Yiddish. He even became friendly with one of the troupe's members and tried to promote the troupe by securing introductions for it and writing favorable reviews of its work. It has been suggested that both the tragicomic tone of the Yiddish plays Kafka saw at this time and also the story in one play of an outcast son may have influenced him in writing "The Metamorphosis."

Critical Overview

Kafka today is a household word around the world, one of the few writers to have an adjective named after him ("Kafkaesque"), describing the dreamlike yet oppressive atmosphere characteristic of his works. When his writings first appeared, however, some reviewers found them baffling, tedious, or exasperating; and the two extreme ideological movements of the twentieth century both found his message unacceptable. The Nazis banned him, and Communist critics denounced him as decadent and despairing.

But fairly quickly Kafka began to be praised by a host of influential writers and intellectuals. The English poet W. H. Auden compared him to Dante, Shakespeare, and Goethe. The German writer Thomas Mann, quoted by Ronald Gray in his book *Franz Kafka,* said that Kafka's works are "among the worthiest things to be read in German literature." And the philosopher Hannah Arendt, writing during World War II, said (also as quoted by Gray) that "Kafka's nightmare of a world... has actually come to pass."

Kafka's friend Max Brod, one of the earliest commentators on Kafka, saw his works as essentially religious and Jewish, but later commentators have situated Kafka more in the existential, modernist tradition of the first half of the twentieth century, associating him with writers such as Albert Camus and Jean-Paul Sartre, whose works suggest the absurdity and futility of existence.

Among Kafka's works,"The Metamorphosis" is generally considered one of his most representative and also one of his best, along with the novels *The Trial* and *The Castle*.Kafka himself was not always happy with his work, however. In his diary (as quoted in Nahum Glatzer's edition of his stories), he wrote on one occasion that he had "great antipathy" to "The Metamorphosis," calling its ending unreadable. However, "The Metamorphosis" was one of the few works that Kafka made a concerted effort to get published, so he could not have been entirely dissatisfied with it.

In any case, commentators since Kafka have been drawn to the story. By 1973, Stanley Corngold was able to publish a book of summaries of essays on "The Metamorphosis" containing accounts of well over a hundred articles, beginning as early as 1916, when one Robert Miiller described the story as ingenious but implausible. In subsequent years, commentators have generally taken for granted the quality and importance of the story, and have focused on trying to interpret it.

There have been many different and contradictory interpretations. Freudian critics have seen in it a working out of the Oedipal struggle between a father and a son who are rivals for Gregor's mother. Marxist critics, those not simply denouncing Kafka as reactionary, have seen the story as depicting the exploitation of the proletariat. Gregor Samsa has also been seen as a Christ figure who dies so that his family can live.

Critics interested in language and form have seen the story as the working out of a metaphor, an elaboration on the common comparison of a man to an insect. Some critics have emphasized the autobiographical elements in the story, pointing out the similarities between the Samsa household and the Kafkas' while also noting the similarity of the names "Samsa" and "Kafka," a similarity that Kafka himself was aware of, though he said—in a conversation cited in Nahum Glatzer' s edition of his stories—that Samsa was not merely Kafka and nothing else.

Other critics have traced the story's sources back to Fyodor Dostoevsky, Charles Dickens, the Jewish plays that Kafka saw in Prague, and Leopold Von Sacher-Masoch's novel about sado-masochism, *Venus in Furs*.Some have become caught up in taking sides for or against Gregor Samsa. And some have argued that the story is impossible to interpret, which is perhaps why Corngold called his book on the story *The Commentators' Despair*.

But however it is interpreted, the fact that the story has drawn so much attention indicates that it is, as Corngold puts it, "the most haunting and universal of all his stories."

Sources

Corngold, Stanley, *The Commentators' Despair: The Interpretation of Kafka's Metamorphosis,* Kennikat, 1973.

Gray, Ronald, *Franz Kafka,* Cambridge University Press, 1973.

Kafka, Franz, *The Complete Stories and Parables,* edited by Nahum N. Glatzer, Quality Paperback Book Club, 1983.

Further Reading

Bloom, Harold, ed., *Franz Kafka's "The Metamorphosis,"* Chelsea House, 1988.

>This text is a collection of essays analyzing the story.

Brod, Max, *Franz Kafka: A Biography,* translated by G. Humphreys Roberts, Schocken, 1947.

>This book of Kafka's life is told by his friend and literary executor.

Hayman, Ronald, *Kafka: A Biography,* Oxford University Press, 1982.

>Hayman's work is a biographical study that relates Kafka's life to his works.

Pawel, Ernst, *The Nightmare of Reason: A Life of Franz Kafka,* Farrar, Straus & Giroux, 1984.

>This text is a biography of Kafka providing psychological analysis and social background.

9 781375 399968